CREATIVE LIBERATION

Mastering Acrylic Abstract Art for Beginners

Rose Marsha

Table of Contents

CHAPTER ONE

INTRODUCTION

Determined craftsmanship has had something of a terrible addressing a really enormous stretch of time now. Different people can't fight the temptation to consider what the explanation in painting in such a way is when veered from extra illustrative styles of workmanship. Others rebuff sensible craftsmanship over its shady straightforwardness, guaranteeing that even little kids can accomplish practically identical outcomes as a five star theoretical painter. While tastes contrast ordinarily around the board, one thing is undeniably. Excellent craftsmanship is pausing, and the craving to comprehend and endeavor to figure out an acceptable method for doing it with no other person's help are both much pursued by approaching understudies. Finding incredible electronic learning classes on this specific subject could emit an impression of being an exceptional undertaking in itself, yet never dread. In the event that you're excited about getting two or three brushes and getting somewhat turbulent yet don't know unequivocally where anyway you're mentoring, you've come to the best regions.

THE BEST METHOD TO PAINT DYNAMIC WORKMANSHIP

Stage One: Be Capable

This could disrupt some of you. A standard problem sensible craftsmanship is made by specialists who can't draw, have no wise preparation, or who are basically spastic. Significant, different lacking and unskilled individuals really participate in ways to deal with acting that outcome in paint being applied to surfaces in propensities that outcome in unrecognizable symbolism. At any rate, while we could call that practically whatever else, for instance, loosening up, hobbying, spending stuff in the parking spot, or venting, what we don't call it is "painting novel workmanship." Being a speculative master looks like being a legal aide, or the highest point of the state. It's a calling. It requires arranging. You truly need to work at it full time and be committed.

Stage Two: Be Purposeful

This, as well, may come as a blunder however certainly, even determined materials start with a thought. It's an impressive sum more irrationality and stylish to envision uncommon specialists as remarkable animals who channel huge powers that even they do not know, and that their boundless cooperation leads them zombie-like to the material where unexpected powers course through them without their control, and that the subsequent pieces are open to such wild cognizance that all potential repercussions loaded upon them are maybe critical. Notwithstanding, even a short gander at determined workmanship's plan of experiences shows that the converse is significant. With predictable obligation they annihilated painting, isolating parts like tone, line, structure, surface, sparkle, sign, surface and stroke. With objective, they looked for ways to deal with utilizing those parts to give something extensive how makers use parts like tone, outlook, meter and key to pass dynamic universalities on through music.

Stage Three: Be Proper

The present normal for specialists to go straightforwardly from helper school to school, obviously from school to Graduate School, and obviously from graduate school to an expert practice. What sort of workmanship is made by a 25-year old who has never worked a customary work, never been completely committed for covering bills, never kept a home, oversaw delegates, or by and large expected to explore the different weakening complexities attracted with the cutting edge human battle for tirelessness? To be a trained professional, and to have objective in your work, and to be suitable, you should investigate the others. See the world. Travel. Investigate. Figure out a smart method for cooking. Go to a show. Address something. Change your perspective and address something different. Find out about what life resembles for the other 7 billion individuals in the world who could experience your solidarity. These outings straightforwardly brief her sense as for self and her visual language, accomplishing work that feels layered, present day and all over the planet. Handle, speculative craftsmanship shouldn't for even a moment worry about to be "associated with something," yet it ought to be made by somebody who is.

Stage Four: Have an Examination

To be an expert intriguing master, you'll ultimately need to show somebody your work. Watchers will introduce demands like, "Is this picture illustrative of something different, or does it essentially reference itself?" or, "Was this painting showed up at through the purposefully confusing of unmistakable articles, or was it the postponed outcome of normal, nonrepresentational developments?" or, "Why red? Why not blue, and so on. As an expert gifted specialist, you should advance a safeguard considering a genuine worry for what you make. Be sure, and legitimate. There's not a possible choice for sagacious clearness. You don't need to make sense of your work, or get out anything it means or what's continuing on with it. In any case, to decline to understand your presumption, to leave the watcher, or to not convey anything at everything is basically senseless, and gives it for others to depict your work.

Stage Five: Be in Charge

Craftsmanship isn't accidental. Amazing appearances are hit messes up. Each etching that breezes up on the outer layer of a speculative material occurs as the possible result of the activities and decisions of the painter. Whether a painter decides to set a material outer in the downpour, the subsequent watermarks happen as the result of decision.

In addition, in the event that the painter isn't content with an etching, the painter can clean it up, cover it, transform it, or obliterate made by craftsmanship. That is called changing. You work, you change, you work some more. Why look for cover behind the lie of debacles in your work? Thought isn't chaos. All of Own defects on each innovative creation. In the event that something occurs in the work that you hadn't deliberately anticipated, address it. Face the unconstrained occasion and pick whether or not to keep it. Anything you pick, and anything that the work becomes, it will be by decision.

Stage Six: Be Open

Perhaps this step appears, apparently, to be unusual, considering that the beyond five stages beat home the significance of being purposeful, reasonable, and controlled. We're not saying to fail to review all that. We're fundamentally in addition saying to open up. Associate with your psyche. Some spot inside your cerebrum is a complete thing to each individual from humankind. Grant your opinions to facilitate your body. Paint normally. Put your perspectives on the material. Whether what you paint is instinctual, fundamental, unconstrained and free, you are as of now picking. You truly change. You truly pick while the game plan is finished.

Stage Seven: Be Unadulterated

Make yourself some tea. Search in the cup
and say without holding back, "This is tea."
Presently, empty some squeezed orange
into the tea. Thoroughly search in the cup
once more and ask yourself, "What is
this?" Contemporary specialists approach
all of workmanship history. They're
allowed to investigate any style and any
medium, and to mix styles and mediums to
track down their remarkable voice and
satisfy their calculated vision. In any case,
when styles are combined as one, what are
we left with? In the event that you paint a
theoretical monochrome however, glue a
collection of unscripted television stars
over it, will be it actually dynamic? It
contains components of reflection, yet is it

the equivalent? It resembles emptying squeezed orange into your tea. You simply wind up saying, "What is this?" It implies something to call a canvas dynamic. To hold that significance, virtue is vital.

Stage Eight: Be New

As of late we heard a painter portray one more painter's work as "illustrative canvases of dynamic compositions." Beside the humor of the assertion, it raised the point that we're the recipients of over 100 years of unique craftsmanship, and the extraordinary conceptual painters of the twentieth Century achieved to such an extent! To ascend to the level of those incredible specialists who went previously, the present unique painters should track down ways of making work that is new. Indeed, every painter should face the need to some way or another consumes the surface's unfilled space. Furthermore, of the multitude of requests we've made on unique painters up until this point, the extra test to consume that vacant space with something altogether new could appear to be the most overwhelming. Yet, it is this capacity to communicate something new and interesting that is generally imperative to reflection's future. Assuming you follow the other seven stages; in other words in the event that you're capable, purposeful, important, have an assessment, stay in charge, remain open, and endeavor to be unadulterated; you'll not have the option honestly and consistent with yourself. What's more, legitimate self-articulation can't resist the urge to prompt something particularly yours, and by definition, new.

CHAPTER TWO

HOW WOULD YOU JUDGE THE NATURE OF A THEORETICAL ARTISTIC CREATION

To pass judgment on quality dynamic craftsmanship, you should think about a few variables regarding the work of art. These variables will assist you with acquiring a superior comprehension of what makes great quality unique workmanship. It will likewise assist you with concluding whether the workmanship merits the venture.

1. Creation of craftsmanship

Understanding creation in unique craftsmanship is likely perhaps of the main component that would assist you with evaluating the nature of dynamic workmanship. Allow me to make sense of structure momentarily. A theoretical canvas or some other work of art is comprised of a few components, for instance, colors, shapes, structures, lines and surfaces. The arrangement of these components in unambiguous ways is known as the standards of workmanship. The general assortment of the relative multitude of components and their positions on a material, for instance, make up the last piece of craftsmanship.

I have composed three different nitty gritty articles making sense of the components of unique workmanship, the standards of dynamic craftsmanship and the arrangement in conceptual craftsmanship. I'm certain these articles would provide you with a more prominent comprehension of the design of unique fine art. Once more, assuming you really want further clarification, kindly let me in on in the remarks area beneath. You don't need to be an expert conceptual craftsman or a college graduate to dig further into the details of workmanship or unique craftsmanship. Indeed, I concur that some of it very well may be somewhat overpowering for individuals who basically need to appreciate workmanship without essentially the additional difficulties of the craftsmanship world. A very much formed theoretical canvas will promptly provide you with a feeling of congruity and equilibrium. You would see every one of the components appear to fit in pleasantly and serenely. Regardless of whether you know about the specialized side of synthesis, you will feel that everything in that piece of craftsmanship supplements one another and cooperate well. Each component adds to the general synthesis. One of the manners in which I use to assess quality unique workmanship is to look at the nature of creation by taking as much time as necessary viewing at the craftsmanship overall. Taking a gander at how the different components are cooperating. Is there any region of the fine art that vibe unequal or awkward? Are there any components that divert from the general impact of the piece?

One more method for passing judgment on creation is to look nearer and center on individual components. How would they exclusively and by and large add to the general impact? Assuming I take one component out or add another component, how might that influence the equilibrium of the artistic creation?

Is there a reasonable amicable variety range that makes a feeling of solidarity, congruity and equilibrium, or does the utilization of variety feel incoherent or indiscriminate?

You most likely have heard other expert craftsmen or craftsmanship vendors use expressions, for example, 'dynamic' and 'drawing in' bits of workmanship. This is where a skilful craftsman makes quality unique workmanship that brings you into it and holds your consideration for an extensive stretch.

A great unique craftsmanship inspires your feelings and makes a visual language that speaks with you. It very well may be inspiring numerous feelings and sentiments and it very well may be conveying thoughts, convictions or even creative mind. Quality theoretical craftsmanship would do substantially more than bring out feelings and correspondence. It would attempt to associate with you. In the event that you truly do associate with the craftsmanship, you are probably going to encounter a profound reaction or reverberation. The association among you and a piece of craftsmanship is difficult to depict in words. It's an incredible sensation which can be founded on a few things, including individual encounters, social impacts or simply fundamental human motivations.

Individuals cry while standing by listening to astounding profound music or melodies; individuals cry watching miserable motion pictures or perusing miserable books, however on rare occasions we hear individuals cry while survey a work of art.

Artistic creations, especially conceptual are genuinely coming up short on the rundown of expressions that get strong profound reactions. Correspondence, obviously, is a two-way road comprised of three components. The source, the message and the collector.

It is what is happening with quality conceptual workmanship. The craftsman or his/her feelings, the fine art and the watcher's close to home reaction. Quality dynamic craftsmanship can get areas of strength for a reaction in us and act as a device for self-reflection. It addresses all of us in a novel manner. Arrangement is by a long shot the principal key in assessing and deciding the degree of value unique workmanship, well as I would see it.

2. Procedures utilized in workmanship

Quality unique workmanship is made with skilful procedures. It doesn't occur indiscriminately as certain individuals might think. Assessing quality conceptual workmanship methods might be more trying for certain individuals who are not really profound into the specialized side of making craftsmanship.

The procedure shows the craftsman's gifts and excellent quality, for example, the dominance of brushstrokes, variety mixing and layering, among others. The construction and every one of the components of the craftsmanship ought to be steady all through the whole work of art.

The craftsman's capacity to utilize and exhibit these methods really and handily can essentially affect the general nature of the piece. One method for evaluating the nature of unique craftsmanship is to check out intently at the outer layer of the composition. Are there any region where the paint of different materials shows up slim or lopsided, recommending an absence of expertise or experience? Or on the other hand are there regions where the craftsman has involved the materials in a specific successful or imaginative manner, displaying their expertise and imagination? One more method for assessing quality conceptual workmanship is to consider the general impression made by the fine art. Does it feel level or two-layered, or does it have a feeling of profundity and dimensionality? Does the canvas feel static or dormant, or does it have a feeling of energy and development? By giving close consideration to the nature of strategy in conceptual workmanship, you can acquire a more profound appreciation for the expertise and imagination engaged with making exceptional and convincing show-stoppers.

3. Innovation of craftsmanship

Innovation of craftsmanship is so private to the craftsman himself/herself. This recognizes the singular craftsman's style from the wide range of various specialists. With regards to the singular craftsmanship style, it generally helps me to remember our extraordinary individual penmanship style. It's so one of a kind. Creativity, in this specific situation, alludes to the craftsman's capacity to make unmistakable and extraordinary fine art that isn't imitative or subsidiary of different works.

Theoretical craftsmanship, specifically, is known for its accentuation on development and innovation. The craftsman is in many cases working without the requirements of authenticity or portrayal. This fundamental component permits the craftsman to investigate new and unique ways of making appealing workmanship from barely anything. One method for assessing the innovation of value dynamic craftsmanship is to think about the craftsman's general collection of work. Does the craftsman have a special style that is clear across various pieces, or takes care of their responsibilities feel disconnected or conflicting? How can it contrast with different fine arts in a similar sort or style?

4. Feeling and Articulation in workmanship

One more key component to think about while evaluating the general nature of a piece of conceptual craftsmanship is feeling and articulation. The capacity of the craftsmen to depict a particular inclination through their work of art, habitually using tone, structure and surface, is alluded to in this detect as feeling and articulation.

Since the theoretical craftsman is unlimited in their investigation of their own inward sentiments and encounters and isn't expected to portray objects from this present reality, dynamic workmanship is ordinarily connected to summoning feelings and communicating sentiments.

Contingent upon the craftsman's goal and the watcher's translation, the fine art might excite a wide assortment of sentiments, from joy and positive thinking to misery and depression. Variety has a major impact in making various states of mind. Variety brain science assumes a huge part with regards to variety implications and affiliations. These are extremely emotional as they are affected by private experience and social impacts.

Splendid, dynamic tones might bring out a feeling of happiness and fervor, while hazier and more curbed varieties might convey a feeling of despairing or despair.

Surfaces, shapes and lines can likewise assume a part in conveying feeling, with unpleasant, barbed lines proposing hostility or strain, while delicate, streaming lines might give a feeling of quiet and serenity.

5. Materials and Medium utilized in workmanship

Great dynamic workmanship ought to be made utilizing top notch materials. Try not to hope to find quality dynamic workmanship made utilizing inferior quality paints or mediums. It doesn't work by any stretch of the imagination. Indeed, it costs more to purchase great quality paints and mediums. Proficient quality paints are more costly in contrast with lower quality paints. It's not just paints and mediums, you would likewise consider different materials utilized like the outer layer of the composition.

There are many surfaces utilized by specialists to make visual workmanship. The absolute most normal surfaces incorporate paper, material, wood, Masonite, aluminum, copper, and so on. It doesn't stop there. Each kind of surface arrives in a wide range of characteristics that could influence the general nature of the craftsmanship. For instance, a cloth material is considerably more costly than a cotton material because of its solidarity and sturdiness. Quality material in the possession of a skilful craftsman can have an enormous effect between excellent dynamic workmanship and a not all that great craftsmanship. The distinction would be clear even to the undeveloped eyes.

Assessing quality material as well as procedures utilized in making theoretical craftsmanship perhaps presents a test to many individuals. One of the most mind-blowing ways of figuring out more about the nature of methods and materials is to straightforwardly ask the craftsman. Foster a decent compatibility with the craftsman and ask him/her every one of the inquiries you want to explain about the fine art.

CHAPTER THREE

WAYS TO RECOGNIZE QUALITY CONCEPTUAL WORKMANSHIP

Presently we take care of a portion of the vital variables to ponder while assessing quality conceptual workmanship, we should investigate a few explicit tips to help you more in recognizing quality craftsmanship pieces.

• Search for equilibrium and concordance

As I referenced before, quality theoretical workmanship will have a feeling of concordance and harmony between the entireties of its components. Search for pieces that draw your prompt consideration. It very well may be the concordance of the tones, shapes or different components in the fine art that grabbed your eye. A decent quality unique craftsmanship would project total congruity and equilibrium in the general components of the work of art.

Regardless of whether you are curious about workmanship strategies, you would feel it. You would feel that the whole work of art looks and feels agreeable and adjusted. Check out nearer at every one of the components and their singular arrangement in the work of art. Then make a stride back and view at the craftsmanship in general and perceive how the different components cooperate to make a feeling of concordance and equilibrium. Thusly, you can acquire a more profound enthusiasm for the craftsman's expertise and the close to home effect of the workmanship.

• Think about the craftsman's standing

Figure out who is the craftsman behind the piece you are thinking about. Converse with the craftsman straightforwardly, if conceivable. Learn about their degree of involvement, expertise and inventiveness. A notable craftsman with a decent standing is probably going to make top notch fine art that is viewed as important and pursued by gatherers and workmanship lovers. However, it doesn't necessarily need to be a notable craftsman

There are numerous other capable and skilful less popular craftsmen who might deliver similarly great fine art however have not acquired a similar degree of openness or acknowledgment.

Finding and valuing crafted by less popular craftsmen can be an intriguing and remunerating experience for craftsmanship aficionados and gatherers. These specialists might offer a new viewpoint or one of a kind style that isn't as usually found in that frame of mind of additional notable craftsmen. I generally think a piece of craftsmanship is a piece of the craftsman himself/herself.

It's actually quite significant that the craftsman's standing can give important understanding and setting into the nature of their work, yet it ought not to be the sole deciding element in your assessment of value conceptual craftsmanship.

• Take as much time as necessary

The significance of making that special interaction with a piece of workmanship. To permit yourself to make an association and to permit the craftsmanship to maneuver into it, you should permit a lot of opportunity to check it out. I can't put more accentuation on giving yourself a lot of opportunity to draw in your sentiments with the fine art. Indeed, you would be taking a gander at the craftsmanship with your eyes however you need to let your sentiments 'see' it. Do you have at least some idea that a review was completed to check how long exhibition hall guests' spend checking out at a piece of craftsmanship? The response is under 30 seconds. Some say that the normal is 17 seconds.

That truly shocked me a ton. It is absolutely impossible that anyone can appreciate checking out at any artwork in 17 seconds. Whenever I visit a workmanship display or a gallery, I would begin from one end and invest as much energy as I feel happy with checking every individual composition out. Furthermore, it's certainly much more than 17 or 30 seconds. That is not all. This is just the main round. At the point when I have taken a gander at every one of the works of art, I would go briefly round and begin once more. This is the point at which I could be investing pretty much energy taking a gander at each painting once more. This could require a couple of hours, contingent upon the number of bits of craftsmanship that are right there. It doesn't stop there. At the point when I leave the craftsmanship display or historical center, I would contemplate those bits of work of art that pulled in me the most. What was it about that painting? For what reason did it stand out for me? What did I like about it? Etc.

Profound association with a static item could take some time. You should be willing and ready to permit yourself the time and commitment with the fine art that it might merit. Taking as much time as is needed to see the value in craftsmanship doesn't ensure that you will continuously have an association with it. At times it works and once in a while it doesn't.

• Pay attention to your instinct

I left awesome for last. I genuinely accept craftsmanship is a language of sentiments. Whether you are an expert craftsman, an accomplished workmanship purchaser or just someone who is essentially intrigued by workmanship, we as a whole gander at craftsmanship since it could move us. It is that vibe of feeling happy with, having a decent outlook on checking workmanship out. A quality piece of craftsmanship is continuously attempting to interface with us, it attempts to let us know something, to cause us to feel something, to impact us somehow. In the event that you feel all that I referenced before in this blog is somewhat overpowering with workmanship detail, trust your own senses and sentiments. You can't turn out badly with that. Since, toward the day's end, you are purchasing that piece of craftsmanship for yourself, not for any other individual.

THE END

www.ingramcontent.com/pod-product-compliance
Lightning Source LLC
Chambersburg PA
CBHW062306290526
45794CB00006B/2708